Football: Learn to Play Football

The Ultimate Guide to Understand Football Rules, Football Positions, Football Statistics and Watch a Football Game Like a Pro!

Stephen Green

© 2015

Stephen Green Copyright © 2015

Table of Contents

A Football Introduction

The first thing you need to understand to understand football is how the field words. It's your basic to everything else. Let's break it down so that you know everything there is to know about the playing field.

End Zones: At each end of the field there is a ten yard wide area. They're inside the end line.

The Sidelines: These are on each side of the field, and it's a boundary line. Its six foot wide, and it runs from one end zone to the next.

End Lines: You'll find that this is another boundary line, and once again it's six feet wide. It connects to the parallel sidelines. These boundary lines make up the shape.

Yard Lines & Hash Marks: First, you need to know what a hash mark is. They're on both ends of the field. They mark every yard in the hundred yard between goal lines, which you'll learn about next. You'll find that they're connected by a solid white line every fifty yard. They're actually only numbered every ten lines though. It creates a crosshatching of lines. They're commonly referred to as a gridiron, but it's just a nickname.

Goal Line: Here is a line that is eight inches wide, and it's over the end zone at the front. Two pylons flank the end of the goal line.

Goal Posts: You'll find these are what you see on the playing field first, and they stand at the center of the very back ends. Its ten feet high, and they extend upward like a fork. It has a horizontal crossbar.

A Little about the Ball:

This is one of the most important things in football because you can't play without your ball. You'll find that NFL footballs are designed only by one company. It's Wilson Sporting Goods Co. It's an oblong sphere, and it's about eleven inches long, but it can be eleven and a half inches long.

It weighs almost fifteen ounces, and it's a polyurethane bladder that's been inflated and laced up with grid-cord. It's then placed in a cowhide covering. There's a three ply sewed in to make sure it maintains its shape. You'll find that it has a valve linked on one side right through the leather covering, and it'll allow air to go through the football so that it's able to be thrown properly.

A Little about the Game

When playing football or watching it, you'll find that there are four quarters to the game. There's a halftime break between the second and third quarter, and that's where you'll find the all famous halftime show when it comes to the Super Bowl. If by chance the game is at a draw after the four quarters, the game is extended. It's only extended for a small period of fifteen minutes.

However, it doesn't have to go for the full fifteen minutes. The team that scores first will win. It can take roughly three to four hours to complete a full game. The clock is technically stopped by teams when an incomplete pass is thrown, they run out of bounds or a team calls a time out. This extends the game time. Each two minute warnings has the clock frozen as well, and these are done two minutes right before the end in both the second and fourth quarter. You'll find that time outs can be done three times in every half.

A Little about Offense:

On the NFL roster there is a max of fifty-three people. However, you'll find that only eleven players are ever permitted on the field at once. There are three teams within a team on the NFL roster, and that's the offense, defense, and the special teams. You'll find that each has specialized positions, but they also have different sets of skills.

Taking a look at offense, their job is to carry the ball from one side of the field to the other. They need to get it on their opponent's side, and to do this they'll run forward holding the bar or pass it to someone else. There are some basic positons that you should know.

The Quarterback: Commonly referred to as QB, you'll find this is one of the most well-known positions on the team. They can also be called the field general. In football, the quarterback is like the leader.

Receivers: they have to run down the field, catching the ball after the QB has thrown it. It all depends on where they're placed, but they can be tight ends, referred to as LTE/RTE, or they can be a wide receiver (WR).

Offensive Linemen: They're meant to block people from getting to the running backs. They do the same for the QB. There are individual positions though, such as Tackles (LT/RT), Center, and Guards (LG/RG). When the Center, they're in the middle of the line. He brings the ball up, hiking it to the QB. Guards will then flank the center, and outside of the guards is where you'll find the Tackles. There will be two tackles and two guards for each team.

Running Backs: They're meant to get the ball from the QB. Then they take it, running up the field. There are different types of running backs. There is halfback (HB), fullback (FB), and tailback (TB). It all depends on the formation.

A Little about Defense:

When a team doesn't have possession of the ball during the game, then they're on defense. This is where they'll then try to prevent the other side from scoring. These players are going to tackle the other players on the other team, trying to get the ball back. There are basic positions for this to happen.

Defensive Linemen: These are meant to put pressure on the QB for the other team, and they're also meant to block running backs. You'll have three to four defensive linemen on a team. They have individual positions as well such as Nose Tackle (NT), Tackle (LDT/RDT), and Ends (LE/RE). When you're dealing with ends, they're going to be found lined on the outside. They run around the offensive tackles. The Nose Tackle will be over the football, and tackle will be put across from the guards. They try to cut into the offensive line.

Cornerbacks (CB): They're meant to prevent WRs from breaking the passes and taking the ball.

Linebackers: There may be four linemen, but there are two outside linebackers (OLB). There is also a middle linebacker (MLB). With three linemen, there will be two outside and two inside (ILB). They back up the linemen while also covering the receivers. They'll even have runners in the group during some plays.

Safeties: Deep behind other defense players, you'll find the Safeties. They're meant to prevent a long pass or even a run. When dealing with a strong safety, they'll be aligned on the side that has a lot of offensive players occupying it. Free safety will have a middle position that's deep.

A Little about Special Teams:

Special teams are important to the game as well. When a team is chosen to kick the ball, you'll find that the special team will take over this job. You'll find that you have the team's kickers, players who run down the field to tackle people, and even the offensive line. You need to know about these positions as well.

The Placekicker: The placekicker is meant to kick the ball into the goalposts so that they can score points for their team. They also are responsible to kick the ball to the opposing team when the game is started.

Returner: This is right during a kickoff or punt, and they have to catch the ball, running it back as far as they can. The point is to try to score a touchdown when a return is issued.

Punter: This player will free kick the ball, but only if the team he is playing for can't advance the ball down the field.

About the Actual Movement

You still need to know how the ball is moved throughout the game. When it begins, a coin will be flipped. This decides what team will have the opening kickoff. The kickoff is just the start because then they have to battle to see who will take position from the opening kickoff. This means that they're trying to see who will get the ball. There are different ways this can happen.

Taking Possession of the Ball:

Here are all of the ways that a team can take possession of the ball.

Safety: A player can be tackled at the end zone, and this is called safety. This way the other team will receive the ball by getting a free kick.

Turnover on Downs: when the offensive team can't advance the ball ten yards in four downs, then the ball is surrendered to the other team.

Receiving a Kickoff: After the other team scores the opposing team will receive a kickoff. This is also done in each half right at the beginning.

Turnover: When a ball is thrown by a QB and then picked off by the other team it is a turnover. It can also be when a ball is dropped and then recovered by the other team.

Punt: With a punt, the defensive team is preventing the offensive team from moving ten yards in three downs. The offense team will then punt or use free kicks to get the other team on the third down.

Tackling the Most Confusing Concept:

American football is confusing to most people, but you'll find that the distance and down system can leave many people bewildered. It's not as confusing as it may seem at first. Four attempts or downs are awarded to teams that take the football into their possession. They can then try to move the ball, and their goal is to move it ten yards.

If they're able to move it at least ten yards within those four downs, then they'll get another set so that they can go at least another ten yards if they can. It will continue on like this. After each play, the officials will need to then determine how many yards a team has either gained or lost after that play.

That's how the line of scrimmage is determined, and it is a line that is imaginary, but it cuts the field. It shows where the offensive team will start on the next play. There's a ten hard long chain handled by a team of officials sitting sideline, and it shows the ten yard mark that the team will need to reach to get the first down. This chain can be brought onto the field when there's a close play. It'll help to measure the distance. They'll measure between the ten yard mark and the ball.

It can be close. The nose of the ball just needs to touch the bar that the chain is attached to. The team can choose to go for it. They can also choose to use their fourth down, and then they have to either reach that ten yard mark or they're forced to surrender the ball. This isn't how it goes most of the time.

They'll usually choose to punt the ball instead, which forces the opposing team to cover a greater distance and they back up the opposing team. The receiving team has the choice to return that punt. To do this they have to catch it and then proceed to run down the field with it. The team that kicks hopes to kick the ball down, and then they try to tackle the kick returner that belongs to the receiving team. They need to do this before he can come back down.

About Running the Ball

To learn about running the ball you need to know about the goal line of the opponent. It's where the team is progressing towards. Any part of the ball can touch the very edge of the goal line, and it'll then be considered to be in the end zone. The team that scored will then have a touchdown. When you hear someone say it's "broken the plane of the end zone" it means that it's now crossed the goal line.

There are different ways to score points, and after a touch down they can try to run or attempt to pass the ball. This will give them a two point conversion, or they can kick a field goal if they choose. That will give them another point. However, if that team tries for the two point conversion, they have a single chance. No second chances.

After they've scored the touchdown and then did one or the other, they then have to kick the ball to the other team. Only in the case of a safety is this not what happens. They'll get a free kick if they receive the ball on a safety.

About the Officials:

The first thing you need to remember is that there are three teams in each football game. The officiating crew is considered to be the third team. They'll be dressed in uniform. They'll have a shirt with white and black stripes that go vertically and white pants. They may also have a white or black hat. They're meant to enforce the rules. These rules are determined by the committee of the NFL. There are six members of the NFL officiating crew. They all have their own set of responsibilities, as you'll read below.

Umpire: This official rules on conduct as well as equipment of all players. He's positioned behind the line of scrimmage. He's five yard behind it.

Referee: This is one of the most well-known officials, and they're meant to be the final authority. They interpret the rules of the game. They also give the signals, and they make the announcements.

Head Linesman: This official will call infractions of the player's movements. This only happens when they're in line on the line of scrimmage. The Head Linesman will also manage the chain crew, keeping track of all the downs.

Field Judge: They make the calls that have to deal with backs and wide receivers as long as they're on their side of the field. He's also meant to watch the defensive players that are being blocked by the back. He'll say if the player is out of bounds or not, and at the beginning of a play, he'll be twenty yards from the line of scrimmage. He is always on the same side as the Line Judge.

Line Judge: They keep time during the football game. This is so they can backup the clock operator. That's not the only person they back up. They also back the Head Linesman when dealing with the line of scrimmage calls.

Side Judge: They make calls regarding WR and backs as long as they're on his side of the field. He also has to watch all players being blocked by the back. He'll say if someone is or isn't out of bounds, standing twenty yards from the line of scrimmage. He'll be on the same side that the Head Linesman is on.

Back Judge: They make calls regarding the tight end, and they'll make calls regarding the player that the tight end is blocking. He's also going to be the one that keeps the time for when a time out is called, intermission, or the twenty-five second play clock.

Learning about Penalties:

To understand why a player is called out, it's important to understand penalties. The official will throw a yellow flag when an infraction is made, and there are many NFL rules. You'll see the main ones below.

Encroachment: This is where a player has moved into what is considered a neutral area, making contact with an offensive player for the opposite team. This happens before the ball is officially in play. To understand this, you need to understand what a neutral zone is. It's the separation of the offense and defense prior to a play, and it's about the same length as the ball.

Excessive Crowd Noise: A referee has to determine if a crowd is making too much noise. The home team can then be penalized five yards or lose a time out if this happens.

Leaping Rule: A football player can block a kick, but they can't run more than a yard behind the line of scrimmage when they're blocking one. A defensive player can run forward, leaping when blocking a kick. Only if he was aligned one yard of the line of scrimmage when the ball was snapped. They can't run up to the line, leaping to block the kick and land on the other players if he's more than one yard from this line. It will cause a fifteen yard penalty.

Intentional Grounding: Here a QB that's in the pocket will throw the ball away intentionally, trying to avoid being tackled, causing a loss of yards. The pocket is the round shape that is formed by the offensive linemen when they're blocking the quarterback.

Fair Catch: The player will receive a kick or punt, and then he might signal that he won't return the football. He does this by raising his arm into the air. The other players are not able to tackle him at this point, but he can't move from the spot where he's received the ball.

Clipping: This is an illegal block, and it's quite dangerous. This is where the player will take out his opponent from behind.

Tuck Rule: This is when the QB drops the ball as he tries to make a pass. His arms need to be moving forward, and then it's a fumble or an incomplete pass.

All about Instant Replay:

There are about twenty cameras that cover the football game because it is so fast paced. That's why an Instant Replay system was included in the game in 1999. It's meant to help assist the officials. Each camera is placed so that it has a different view. They'll be able to use the cameras to look at questionable calls. However, that doesn't mean that every play can be reviewed.

A coach can challenge the call of an official at certain times. They have to toss a red flag into the field. They can only challenge twice per game. If the team doesn't win the challenge, then the team loses a time out and the official's call will stand. If they do win the challenge, then the call of the official is then overruled and the time out will be retained. It has to be made before the next play is started, but a challenge cannot be issued in the last two minutes of either half. However, you'll find that a review can be initiated within overtime period and within the last two minutes of a play. Only be an official replay assistant though.

A replay assistant can request as many replays as they want. The referee only has a minute and a half after a play has been challenged to finish reviewing it. He has a field level monitor to do it. They can review a play that is an incomplete, pass complete or intercepted pass, scoring plays, recovery of a loose ball, when it's out of bounds, illegal passes, number of players on a field and more.

Officials have well-trained eyes, but that doesn't mean they're always correct. They're meant to make the right decision as much as possible. Watch as many games as you can if you want to enjoy it because you need to be familiar with all the terms. Everything may be confusing at first, but it should clear up over time.

Safety in Regards to Football

This is a full contact sport, so injuries aren't uncommon. Luckily, most of the injuries don't occur during the game. They occur during training for the game, but it's kept to a minimum. The players all have equipment that is meant to prevent or at least minimize all injuries. They have a helmet no matter what, but they're also meant to have good shoulder pads.

Other leagues might call for more padding, such as mouth guards, chest protectors, knee pads, and thigh pads as well as guards. Lower extremities are more commonly hurt than upper ones, and knees get hurt quite frequently. However, that doesn't mean that upper extremities aren't affected.

Bruises, sprains, strains, fractures, dislocations, and concussions are some of the most common injuries for a player. A player can even develop chronic traumatic encephalopathy from reoccurring concussions. It can also cause other mental issues, including Parkinson's disease, dementia and even depression.

Helmet contact between opposing players can case a concussion easily, but upper body contact can cause it as well. Though, helmets still help tremendously to prevent serious injuries such as fractures to the skull. There are various programs that have been put into place to try and minimize the concussions that are caused by helmet to helmet contact. Never forget that no matter how entertaining, football is a dangerous sport. Players know the risk that they are taking on when they play, but luckily with proper equipment the damage and risk is minimized.

How to Throw a Football

With this chapter you're going to learn how to throw a football, and soon it'll become quick and easy. You may have to practice, but after a while you shouldn't even have to think about it. It'll be simple and easy, and you'll get the perfect throw every time if you follow these steps.

Step #1 Get a Grip

You need to do what's comfortable on your hands, but your fingers needs to be on the laces. You can put your thumb right at the end of the area that's laced, or you can make a finger-to-lace configuration just for you. Some people won't use the laces, but it's advised that you do if you want to throw like a pro.

If you're unsure how you're going to throw it, just throw it up and catch it again and again. It'll help you to learn where your hands naturally want to grip the ball, and you can work from there to find out exactly how to throw it for you. You want to make a snap and be able to release accurately but also quickly.

Step #2 Get in Stance

Your stance matters as well, and so you'll need to pay attention to your footwork. Make sure that your feet are just slightly more than shoulder width apart, and then, assuming you're right handed, your left foot needs to be forward. Do the opposite if you're left handed. There is an eighty-twenty rule you need to utilize.

Eighty percent of your weight should be placed on the back leg, and twenty percent should be placed on the front. You will gradually switch this as you throw. You should never have all of your weight on one foot. It'll throw your balance. This will mess up your timing as well as your accuracy.

Step #3 Throwing It

When starting your throw, it's best to have the ball over your shoulder, and it should be level with your ear. Keep the ball high when in this position to help you develop a quicker release. You need to release the ball higher, which can avoid defensive linemen knockdowns.

Both hand should be on the ball to keep it secure, and when you're ready to actually throw it, your front arm swings forward and down. Your hips and stomach should be turned into the throw as you step in the right direction. When you release the ball, your thumb should always point towards the ground to finish it.

Some Football Statistics

To understand football a little better, it's best to take a look at player statistics. Let's start with some offensive leaders of right now.

Top Passing Yards:

Philips Rivers: From the San Diego Chargers, passing is 2,116 on average.

Andy Dalton: 1761 Average, CIN

Matty Ryan: 1751 Average, ATL

Carson Palmer: 1737 Average, ARI

Tom Brady: 1699 Average, NE

Top Rushing Yards:

Matt Forte: from the Chicago Bears with a 507 rushing average.

Devonta Freeman: 505 Average, ATL

Carlos Hyde: 470 Average, SF

Chris Ivory: 460 Average, NYJ

Justin Forsett: 457 Average, BAL

Top Receiving Yards:

DeAndre Hopkins: 726 Receiving Average from Houston Texas.

Julio Jones: 638 Average, ATL

Keenan Allen: 601 Average, SD

Larry Fitzgerald: 583 Average, ARI

Antonio Brown: 547 Average, PIT

Top Defensive Leaders Currently:

Top Sacks Yards:

Michael Bennet: 6.5 Average from the Seattle Seahawks

Carlos Dunlap: 6.5 Average, CIN

Chandler Jones: 5.5 Average, NE

Julius Peppers: 5.5 Average, GB

Ezekiel Ansah: 5 Average, DET

Interception Yards:

Mike Adams: 4 Average from the Indianapolis Colts

Josh Norman: 4 Average, CAR

Charles Woodson: 4 Average, OAK

Kenneth Acker: 3 Average, SF

Tramaine Brock: 3 Average, SF

Tackles Yards:

D'Qwell Jackson: 71 Average, Indianapolis Colts

NaVorrow Bowman: 69 Average, SF

Michael Wilhoite: 63 Average, SF

TElvin Smith: 59 Average, JAC

Vincent Rey: 57 Average, CIN

Some More Statistics:

Scoring:

Steven Hauschka: Kicker, SEA, 62 Average

Brandon McManus: Kicker, DEN, 61 Average

Devonta Freeman: Running Back, 60 Average, ATL

Stephen Gostkowski: Kicker, 57 Average, NE

Justin Tucker: Kicker, 53 Average, BAL

Touchdowns:

Devonta Freeman: Running Back, 10 Average, ATL

Tyler Eifert: Tight End, 6 Average, CIN

Larry Fitzgerald: Wide Receiver, 6 Average, ARI

Jeremy Hill: Running Back, 6 Average, CIN

David Johnson: Running Back, 6 Average, ARI

Field Goals:

Brandon McManus: Kicker, 16 Average, DEN

Steven Hauschka: Kicker, 16 Average, SEA

Robbie Gould: Kicker, 15 Average, CHI

Justin Tucker: Kicker, 13 Average, BAL

Josh Brown: Kicker, 12 Average, NYG

Punting:

Jon Ryan: Punter, 1711 Average, SEA

Colton Schmidt: Punter, 1601 Average, BUF
Bradley Pinion: Punter, 1521 Average, SF
Bryan Pinion: Punter, 1505 Average, JAC
Donnie Jones: Punter, 1486 Average, PHI

Punt Returns:

Travis Benjamin: Wide Receiver, 250 Average, CLE
Darren Sproles: Running Back, 204 Average, PHI
Bobby Rainey: Running Back, 199 Average, TB
Jarvis Landry: Wide Receiver, 191 Average, MIA
Tyler Lockett: Wide Receiver, 183 Average, SEA

Kick Returns:

Rashad Ross: Wide Receiver, 352 Average, WAS
Tyler Lockett: Wide Receiver, 338 Average, SEA
David Johnson: Running Back, 327 Average, ARI
Ameer Abdullah: Running Back, 306 Average DET
Knile Davis: Running Back, 251 Average, KC

Tips for Watching Football

Watching football can be complicated at first, but you'll slowly get the hang of it after a while. However, these tips and tricks will help you to understand this game and start enjoying it a lot sooner.

Tip #1 Start with the Line of Scrimmage

You should start by looking wide to see how many receivers you can spot, and then take note of where they're located currently. You can then scan to see how many players are lined on the defensive backfield and the defensive line. You can determine what the play might be when you look at how the players are lined up.

Tip #2 Check on the QB

You may notice that the quarterback is positioned five yards right behind the center, and this means he's in shotgun formation. It's extremely likely that he'll pass the ball in this position. However, there is an unlikely chance that the QB may drop back, handing the ball off to a RB.

Tip #3 Check on Game Progress

Look at the upper corner of your TV screen, and you'll want to take note of what the down is. This will also show you have far the offense has to go for their first down, how much time is currently left on the clock, and it'll tell you the score. If you look at the time left on the clock and the score, you may be able to figure out if a team will pass or run.

Tip #4 Look for Movement

You'll want to look for movement. Look towards the defensive backs and the linebackers. If the defenders are creeping towards the line of scrimmage, it means they're probably going to blitz the QB or they're going to fill the running lanes in an attempt to neutralize a run play.

Tip #5 Count the Defensive Backs

If there are four or more defensive backs in the game, then they're trying to prevent a pass completion.

Tip #6 Pay Attention to Defensive Fronts & Defensive Tackles

If there are only three linemen close to the line of scrimmage, then the defense is most likely expecting the offense to pass the ball. If there are four down linemen on the field and the LBs are within a few yards of the line of scrimmage, they expect the offense to try and run.

Tip #7 Don't Watch the Ball

If you want to watch football like a pro, then you can't keep your eye on the ball. Coaches have to watch more than the ball, and if you're looking at the ball, then you're missing most of the action at any given play. You need to watch how the defense sets up, how they offense then reacts, and you need to watch individual players as they perform their duties. So don't develop tunnel vision on the ball, check out offensive and defensive lines, watch secondary movements, RBs, and receivers.

What to Look For in a Game

You need to know what to look for in a game when you're watching, and even though the tips in the previous chapter will get you started, they aren't always enough. These questions will help you to understand the game, but to get the right answers you need to know what you're supposed to be paying attention to in the first place. Sometimes knowing the basics isn't good enough if you don't know what to pay attention to.

When Watching the Offense:

Always check to see if they tip their hands or if the tackles are set up differently on different pass plays.

Check if the QB read the defense, and do they make a play call based on what they read?

You need to check how they're throwing on a first down. Is it a lot or a little?

Ask yourself how effective their play action is.

Does the receiver bait the secondary?

Look to see if you can see a lean forward made by the limen when rushing play.

Is the motion to set up another play?

When Watching the Defense:

Can the linebackers execute blitz disguise?

Are they crashing? Is the defensive end playing his contain role?

Are the defenders rotating into various coverage packages?

Is the secondary showing a zone look or man-to-man?

Ask yourself how many players are actually on the line.

Are the CBs trying to take away the slant pattern by playing inside the receiver's shoulders?

Is there an overload of defensive players on a side?

When Looking at Field Position:

Do they make a pass play to the end zone inside the opponent's twentyofive yard line on the first down?

With the QB throw deep with the offense backed up? Or will he run the ball and play it safe?

Is there a fake punt? Do you think it'll happen in opponent's territory or midfield?

Look to see if the offensive approach changes depending on where they have the ball positioned.

Making the Call:

When you watch the same team often enough, you're more likely to learn their tendencies. You're most likely going to make calls when you're with your friends watching a game, and when you learn to ask the right questions, it's easier to predict what they're going to do. This will help you to impress your friends by making a better prediction.

NFL Leagues & Conferences

You're probably now curious about the different leagues and a little about them. You'll learn which leagues in the NFL play in what conference, including if it's the American Football League (AFC) or the National Football League (NFC). Below, you'll even find the city that they play in.

Arizona Cardinals:

The Arizona Cardinals have sixty-three players, and here's there positional spending of the cornerback, quarterback, and left tackle.

QB: There are 3, the NFL rank is 16, and the cap dollars for 2015 is $11,834,168.

CB: There are 4, the NFL rank is 6, and the Cap Dollars for 2015 is $21,137,105

LT: There are 2, the NFL rank is 7, and the cap is $9,260,000.

Conference: NFC West

City: Glendale, Arizona

Atlanta Falcons:

They have sixty players, and here's their positional spending.

QB: There are 2, the NFL rank is 4, and the cap dollars for 2015 is $20,096,474.

CB: There are 5, the NFL rank is 27, and the cap dollars for 2015 is $5,464,023.

LT: There are 2, the NFL rank is 18, and the cap dollars for 2015 is $5,008,978.

Conference: NFC South

City: Atlanta, Georgia

Baltimore Ravens:

They have sixty-six players, and here's their positional spending.

QB: There are 2, the NFL rank is 11, and the cap dollars for 2015 is $16,550,000.

CB: There are six, the NFL rank is 11, and the cap dollars for 2015 is $15,939,265.

LT: There are two, the NFL rank is 9, and the cap dollars for 2015 is $8,213,000.

Conference: North AFC

City: Owings Mills, Maryland

Buffalo Bills:

They have sixty-four players, and here's their positional spending.

QB: There are 3, the NFL rank is 30, and the cap dollars for 2015 is $3,719,538.

CB: There are 5, the NFL rank is 25, and the cap dollars for 2015 is $7,041,614.

LT: There are 2, the NFL rank is 27, and the cap dollars for 2015 is $1,975,070.

Conference: AFC East

City: Orchard Park, New York

Carolina Panthers:

There are sixty players, and here's their positional spending.

QB: There are 3, the NFL rank is 14, and the cap dollars for 2015 is $15,429,000.

CB: There are 4, the NFL rank is 31, and the cap dollars for 2015 is $4,472,750.

LT: There are 1, the NFL rank is 26, and the cap dollars for 2015 is $2,421,975.

Conference: NFC South

City: Charlotte, North Carolina

Chicago Bears:

There are sixty-three players, and here's their positional spending.

QB: There are 2, the NFL rank is 9, and the cap dollars for 2015 is $17,625,000.

CB: There are 6, the NFL rank is 24, and the cap dollars for 2015 is $7,243,061.

LT: There are 3, the NFL rank is 6, and the cap dollars for 2015 is $9,018,980.

Conference: NFC North

City: Chicago, Illinois

Cincinnati Bengals:

They have fifty-eight players, and here is their positional spending.

QB: There are 2, the NFL rank is 18, and the cap dollars for 2015 is $10,155,413.

CB: There are 6, the NFL rank is 9, and the cap dollars for 2015 is $17,850,497.

LT: There are 2, the NFL rank is 10, and the cap dollars for 2015 is $7,974,458.

Conference: AFC North

City: Cincinnati, Ohio

Cleveland Browns:

They have sixty-one players, and here is their positional spending.

QB: There are 3, the NFL rank is 25, and the cap dollars for 2015 is $6,758,013.

CB: There are 6, the NFL rank is 2, and the cap dollars for 2015 is $23,780,608.

LT: There is 1, the NFL rank is 4, and the cap dollars for 2015 is $10,200,000.

Conference: AFC North

City: Cleveland, Ohio

Dallas Cowboys:

They have sixty players, and here is their positional spending.

QB: There are 3, the NFL rank is 31, and the cap dollars for 2015 is $3,007,057.

CB: There are 5, the NFL rank is 4, and the cap dollars for 2015 is $21,508,058.

LT: There are 2, the NFL rank is 17, and the cap dollars for 2015 is $5,589,588.

Conference: NFC East

City: Arlington, Texas

Denver Broncos:

They have fifty-seven players, and here is their positional spending.

QB: There are 3, the NFL rank is 7, and the cap dollars for 2015 is $19,067,139.

CB: There are 5, the NFL rank is 14, and the cap dollars for 2015 is $12,765,123.

LT: There are 3, the NFL rank is 25, and the cap dollars for 2015 is $2,601,028.

Conference: AFC West

City: Denver, Colorado

Detroit Lions:

They have fifty-nine players, and here is their positional spending.

QB: There are 2, the NFL rank is 8, and the cap dollars for 2015 is $18,386,250.

CB: There are 5, the NFL rank is 29, and the cap dollars for 2015 is $4,706,521.

LT: There are 2, the NFL rank is 21, and the cap dollars for 2015 is $2,992,927.

Conference: NFC North

City: Denver Colorado

Green Bay Packers:

They have fifty-nine players, and here is their positional spending.

QB: There are 3, the NFL rank is 5, and the cap dollars for 2015 is $19,940,908.

CB: There are 5, the NFL rank is 17, and the cap dollars for 2015 is $11,768,574.

LT: There is 1, the NFL rank is 31, and the cap dollars for 2015 is $698,850.

Conference: NFC North

City: Green Bay, Wisconsin

Houston Texans:

They have sixty-four players, and here's their positional spending.

QB: There are 2, the NFL rank is 21, and the cap dollars for 2015 is $8,406,250.

CB: There are 7, the NFL rank is 3, and the cap dollars for 2015 is $23,041,959.

LT: There are 2, the NFL rank is 5, and the cap dollars for 2015 is $9,935,666.

Conference: AFC South

City: Houston, Texas

Indianapolis Colts:

They have fifty-nine players, and here's their positional spending.

QB: There are 2, the NFL rank is 17, and the cap dollars for 2015 is $10,034,363.

CB: There are 5, the NFL rank is 5, and the cap dollars for 2015 is $20,526,568.

LT: There is 1, the NFL rank is 15, and the cap dollars for 2015 is $6,800,000.

Conference: AFC South

City: Indianapolis, Indiana

Jacksonville Jaguars:

They have sixty-two players, and here's their positional spending.

QB: There are 2, the NFL rank is 20, and the cap dollars for 2015 is $8,194,275.

CB: There are 5, the NFL rank is 22, and the cap dollars for 2015 is $8,936,089.

LT: There are 2, the NFL rank is 14, and the cap dollars for 2015 is $6,577,254.

Conference: AFC South

City: Jacksonville, Florida

Kansas City Chiefs:

They have sixty-one players, and here's their positional spending.

QB: There are 3, the NFL rank is 3, and the cap dollars for 2015 is $20,963,606.

CB: There are 5, the NFL rank is 18, and the cap dollars for 2015 is $10,568,062.

LT: There is 1, the NFL rank is 30, and the cap dollars for 2015 is $844,375.

Conference: AFC West

City: Kansas City, Kansas

Miami Dolphins:

They have fifty-six players, and here is their positional spending.

QB: There are 2, the NFL rank is 24, and the cap dollars for 2015 is $7,473,364.

CB: There are 5, the NFL rank is 12, and the cap dollars for 2015 is $14,146,022.

LT: There are 2, the NFL rank is 1, and the cap dollars for 2015 is $11,682,500.

Conference: AFC East

City: Miami Gardens, Florida

Minnesota Vikings:

They have sixty players, and here is their positional spending.

QB: There are 3, the NFL rank is 28, and the cap dollars for 2015 is $5,245,038.

CB: There are 6, the NFL rank is 15, and the cap dollars for 2015 is $12,984,479.

LT: There is 1, the NFL rank is 16, and the cap dollars for 2015 is $6,290,644.

Conference: NFC North

City: Minneapolis, Minnesota

New England Patriots:

They have sixty-three players, and here is their positional spending.

QB: There are 2, the NFL rank is 15, and the cap dollars for 2015 is $14,791,795.

CB: There are 4, the NFL rank is 32, and the cap dollars for 2015 is $2,103,754.

LT: There is 1, the NFL rank is 24, and the cap dollars for 2015 is $2,616,666.

Conference: AFC East

City: Foxborough, Massachusetts

New Orleans Saints:

They have sixty-one players, and here is their positional spending.

QB: There are 3, the NFL rank is 1, and the cap dollars for 2015 is $25,083,291.

CB: There are 6, the NFL rank is 23, and the cap dollars for 2015 is $8,997,473.

LT: There are 2, the NFL rank is 28, and the cap dollars for 2015 is $1,216,711.

Conference: NFC South

City: New Orleans, Louisiana

New York Giants:

They have sixty-three players, and here is their positional spending.

QB: There are 2, the NFL rank is 13, and the cap dollars for 2015 is $15,148,400.

CB: There are 7, the NFL rank is 7, and the cap dollars for 2015 is $17,870,720.

LT: There is 1, the NFL rank is 23, and the cap dollars for 2015 is $2,616,676.

Conference: NFC East

City: East Rutherford, New Jersey

New York Jets:

They have sixty players, and here is their positional spending.

QB: There are 3, the NFL rank is 29, and the cap dollars for 2015 is $5,192,407.

CB: There are 6, the NFL rank is 1, and the cap dollars for 2015 is $28,009,719.

LT: There are 2, the NFL rank is 2, and the cap dollars for 2015 is $12,458,666.

Conference: AFC East

City: East Rutherford, New Jersey

Oakland Raiders:

They have fifty-eight players, and here is their positional spending.

QB: There are 2, the NFL rank is 32, and the cap dollars for 2015 is $1,805,864.

CB: There are 6, the NFL rank is 26, and the cap dollars for 2015 is $5,619,938.

LT: There are 2, the NFL rank is 12, and the cap dollars for 2015 is $7,150,000.

Conference: AFC West

City: Oakland California

Philadelphia Eagles:

They have fifty-eight players, and here is their positional spending.

QB: There are 3, the NFL rank is 12, and the cap dollars for 2015 is $17,251,176.

CB: There are 5, the NFL rank is 13, and the cap dollars for 2015 is $13,507,248.

LT: There is 1, the NFL rank is 8, and the cap dollars for 2015 is $9,050,000.

Conference: NFC East

City: Philadelphia, Pennsylvania

Pittsburgh Steelers:

They have sixty-seven players, and here is their positional spending.

QB: There are 3, the NFL rank is 6, and the cap dollars for 2015 is $18,524,805.

CB: There are 5, the NFL rank is 16, and the cap dollars for 2015 is $12,166,668.

LT: There are 1, the NFL rank is 32, and the cap dollars for 2015 is $435,000.

Conference: AFC North

City: Pittsburgh, Pennsylvania

San Diego Chargers:

They have fifty-nine players, and here is their positional spending.

QB: There are 2, the NFL rank is 2, and the cap dollars for 2015 is $22,989,168.

CB: There are 5, the NFL rank is 21, and the cap dollars for 2015 is $9,201,549.

LT: There is 1, the NFL rank 20, and the cap dollars for 2015 is $4,125,000.

Conference: AFC West

City: San Diego, California

San Francisco 49ers:

They have fifty-eight players, and here is their positional spending.

QB: There are 2, the NFL rank is 10, and the cap dollars for 2015 is $17,015,753.

CB: There are 4, the NFL rank is 30, and the cap dollars for 2015 is $4,341,486.

LT: There is 1, the NFL rank is 11, and the cap dollars for 2015 is $7,600,000.

Conference: NFC West

City: Santa Clara, California

Seattle Seahawks:

They have sixty players, and here is their positional spending.

QB: There are 2, the NFL rank is 22, and the cap dollars for 2015 is $8,554,868.

CB: There are 5, the NFL rank is 8, and the cap dollars for 2015 is $18,363,229.

LT: There is 1, the NFL rank is 13, and the cap dollars for 2015 is $7,280,000.

Conference: NFC West

City: Seattle, Washington

St. Louis Rams:

They have fifty-six players, and here is their positional spending.

QB: There are 3, the NFL rank is 27, and the cap dollars for 2015 is $5,218,449.

CB: There are 4, the NFL rank is 28, and the cap dollars for 2015 is $4,955,846.

LT: There is 1, the NFL rank is 19, and the cap dollars for 2015 is $4,837,295.

Conference: NFC West

City: St. Louis, Missouri

Tampa Bay Buccaneers:

They have fifty-eight players, and here is their positional spending.

QB: There are 3, the NFL rank is 26, and the cap dollars for 2015 is $5,965,886.

CB: There are 6, the NFL rank is 20, and the cap dollars for 2015 is $8,832,232.

LT: There is 1, the NFL rank is 29, and the cap dollars for 2015 is $1,103,429.

Conference: NFC South

City: Tampa, Florida

Tennessee Titans:

They have fifty-nine players, and here is their positional spending.

QB: There are 3, the NFL rank is 23, and the cap dollars for 2015 is $7,443,820.

CB: There are 5, the NFL rank is 10, and the cap dollars for 2015 is $14,810,105.

LT: There is 1, the NFL rank is 22, and the cap dollars for 2015 is $2,610,228.

Conference: AFC South

City: Nashville, Tennessee

Washington Redskins:

They have sixty-two players, and here is their positional spending.

QB: There are 3, the NFL rank is 19, and the cap dollars for 2015 is $8,872,885.

CB: There are 5, the NFL rank is 19, and the cap dollars for 2015 is $10,396,352.

LT: There are 2, the NFL rank is 3, and the cap dollars for 2015 is $11,190,388.

Conference: NFC East

City: Landover, Maryland

An Easy Glossary

Extra Point: This is a kick that is worth a single point. It's attempted after a touchdown. It can also be called point after touchdown (PAT).

Fair Catch: When a player returns a punt, waving his arm from side to side over his head. This player cannot run with the ball after signaling. Those attempting to tackle, must desist.

Drive: This is the series of plays that happens when the offense has possession of the ball. The other team will get possession when they punt or score.

Fumble: This is where someone loses the ball when being tackled or running. You can recover a fumble if you're a member of the defense or offense. It's called a turnover when the defense recovers it.

Field Goal: This is a kick that is worth three points, and it can be attempted at any position on the field. However, it is usually attempted when the player is within forty yards of the goalpost. It must sail above the crossbar, like an extra point, and it must go through the uprights of the goalpost.

Huddle: This is where eleven of the players on the field meet up together, discussing strategies. It happens between plays. When on offense, the QB will relay the plays during this time.

Handoff: This is where one player gives the ball to another. Usually the QB gives it to the RB, but this is not necessary to be a handover.

Incompletion: This is where they attempt a forward pass but it falls to the ground because the receiver is unable to catch it. It can also be where the receiver dropped it or even caught it out of bounds.

Kickoff: This is a free kick, which means the team receiving can't attempt to block it. It puts the ball into play, and it's used when the first and third quarters are started, and it's done after every touchdown or successful field goal.

Interception: This is where a defensive player catches the pass.

Offensive Line: This is the five men who make up a human wall to block for as well as protect the QB as well as ball carriers. Each line will have a center, and this is who snaps the ball. It also has two tackles and two guards.

Red Zone: This is an unofficial area of the field, and it's from the twenty yard line all the way to the opponent's goal line. It's considered to be a moral victor in the defense's favor when they can hold the opponent to a field goal in the red zone.

Punt: This is another kick, and it's made when a player has dropped the ball, kicking it while it falls towards the foot. It's commonly made on the fourth down when the offense is forced to surrender their possession of the ball to the defense. This happens because they couldn't advance ten yards.

Rushing: This is where the ball is advanced by running. It does not include passing.

Return: This is where the players receives the punt or kick, running it towards the opponent's goal line. They're intent on gaining significant yardage or scoring if they can.

Safety: This is a type of score that equals two points. The defense earns this by tackling an offensive player that has the ball in their own end zone.

Sack: This is where a defensive player will tackle the QB. It's done behind the line of scrimmage, and it results in a loss of yardage.

Snap: This is where the ball is hiked, which is tossed between the legs, to the QB. It's performed by the center, but it can also be done to the holder when they're performing a kick attempt or to the punter. The ball is in play officially when a snap occurs, and it's in action when it begins.

Secondary: This includes four defensive players, defending against the pass as well as line up behind the LB, and the wide on the corner that is opposite the receiver.

Touchdown: This is a score that is worth six points, and it occurs when a player has the ball and crosses the opponent's goal line. It can also be when they catch the ball while they're in their opponent's end zone, or even when the defensive player recovers a loose ball in that end zone.

Conclusion

Thank you again for downloading this book!

I hope this book was able to help you to learn more about NFL leagues, how to throw a football, and watch a football game successfully.

The next step upon successful completion of this book is to start watching more games and put into practice all the knowledge you've just been equipped with.

Thank you and good luck!

CPSIA information can be obtained
at www.ICGtesting.com
Printed in the USA
LVOW04s0355020816
498623LV00032B/1274/P

9 781519 767493